In the afternoon

by Beverley Randell
Photography by Bill Thomas

one o'clock

It is one o'clock
in the afternoon.
It is time
for a story.
Our teacher
reads to us.

Then we paint pictures.

two o'clock

It is time
for singing.
I sing a song
with my friends.

After that,
we go outside
to play
some games.

 three o'clock

It is time to go home.
My grandma comes to school
to meet me,
and I walk home with her.

four o'clock

It is time
to have
something
to eat
and drink.

My big sister comes home,
and we go outside to play.

five o'clock

It is time for Mom
to come home
from work.
We run to meet her.

Then we watch television.

 six o'clock

It is time for dinner.
I set the table.
We will all sit down to eat
when Dad comes home.

seven o'clock

It is time
to brush
my teeth again,
and then
it is time
for my bath.

My dad reads me
a bedtime story.

I love stories.

eight o'clock

It is time
to go
to bed.